Do You Have It?

By: Dr. Ruth M. Wilson

BK Royston Publishing

Jeffersonville, IN

BK Royston Publishing
P. O. Box 4321
Jeffersonville, IN 47131
502-802-5385
http://bkroystonpublishing.com

© Copyright – 2015

All Rights Reserved. No part of this book may be reproduced, stored in a retrieval system, or transmitted by any means without the written permission of the author.

Cover DESIGNER: TED DONES
TLD GRAPHIC DESIGN
417.396.8295 | P.O.BOX 43881
LOUISVILLE, KY 40243
WWW.MESSENGERSOFFIRE.ORG

ISBN-13: 978-0692610077
ISBN-10: 0692610073

All Scriptures are taken from the KING JAMES VERSION (KJV): public domain or from the version of the bible listed and within the permission for use guidelines.

Printed in the United States of America

Dedication

In loving memory of my dad, Walter Wilson, Jr. and my Grandmothers, Ruth Hampton and Nellie Marie Curry, All of Whom had "It."

This book is dedicated to the Queen of talk show hosts.

"You have It!" I heard it not only through my ears but also in my soul and was inspired to write. May the words you spoke that night to your daughter and the words I've written be life, be a blessing and a source of strength, to all that read, hear and receive them.

"He sent his word, and healed them. And delivered them from their destructions." Psalms 107:20 (KJV)

Introduction

This book was written to strengthen, heal, encourage, uplift, inspire and ignite you to walk into your destiny. Sometimes the travels of life can be so devastating and discouraging that we become stagnate or imprisoned in our past. I want you to know today, my sister, my brother, that no matter what you've done, no matter what you've been through, no matter what anybody has said or saying to you, YOU ARE SPECIAL, YOU ARE SOMEBODY, YOU HAVE A GOD GIVEN PURPOSE TO MAKE A DIFFERENCE IN THIS LIFE AND THIS WORLD.

There is an abundance of wealth with your name on it, waiting on your arrival at DESTINY. Go get it!

YOU HAVE "IT"

Again, don't allow people, your past, or your present situation to determine your future, you can do it!

Read this book every day for 30 days or until it becomes life to you then step out on faith and begin your walk to DESTINY!

"I know the plan I have for," announces the Lord. I want you to enjoy success. I do not plan to harm you. I will give you hope for the years to come."
Jeremiah 29:11 (NIRV)

Foreword

The difference between successful people and non-successful people has been often called the "IT" Factor. When you watch an award show, see an interview or admire the display of any celebrity or someone of notoriety, you wonder what really sets them apart from me. What do they have that I don't have? Why are they in that position and I am not? What were they willing to do that I am not or do not even know how to do to be successful?

Dr. Ruth Wilson has given us specific keys to natural as well as spiritual success. She explains that this is a process, a commitment and you must be disciplined with using these keys on a daily basis. First, I encourage you to decide, do you even want "IT?" Then, how bad do you want

"IT?" Once you have answered these two questions, turn the page to determine what it will take to get "IT!"

Be blessed.

Dr. Julia A. Royston

What is IT?

It is
Inner Strength

Self-confidence that stands up within me, assuring me that I can do whatever I set my heart to.

It is self-assurance that if I believe in myself nothing and no one can hold me down, hold me back or keep me quiet.

It is that positive self-image that allows me to see myself as God sees me perfect, and lacking nothing.

It is power and might inside me that makes me breathe when life is trying to choke me. It is that same power and might that makes me get back up every time life knocks me down.

I refuse to be weak. I refuse to be limited.

"I can do all things through Christ which strengthens me."
Philippians 4:13 (KJV)

Discouraging voices only have the power that you give them.

It is
Determination

It is the, I MUST do this, inside me that pushes me every day to excel, to accomplish more today than I did yesterday. It is perseverance, immovability that shouts, "I MUST!" I will stay focused on what I am doing because I cannot afford to be distracted or taken off course.

It is dedication, my faithfulness, my allengiance, my devotion and loyalty to my purpose.

It is walking against a boisterous wind called life with everything that I have.

I refuse to be indifferent and unfaithful to myself.

"Be ye strong therefore, and let not your hands be weak: for your work shall be rewarded."
2 Chronicles 15:7 (KJV)

The tree's ability to withstand any strength of wind is based on the strength of the tree's roots. A man's ability to withstand any circumstance or condition is based on the strength of that man's mind.

_____
_____
_____
_____
_____
_____
_____
_____
_____
_____
_____
_____
_____
_____

It is Discipline

Self-control, making sure that I do only what I am supposed to do, when I am supposed to do it, those things that guarantee my success. It is self-denial abstaining, avoiding, renouncing, anything and anyone that would distract me, take me off course, and abort my destiny.

It is the ability to stay focused, to run in this race called life and cross the finish line of purpose and destiny, which equal success.

I refuse to be disorganized, lazy and intoxicated by the things of this world.

"Know ye not that they which run in a race run all, but one receive the prize? So run, that ye may obtain."
I Corinthians 9:24 (KJV)

If you only give your time, energy and strength to moving forward, you don't have to worry about being left behind.

It is Endurance

Continuing, lastingness, permanence, stability.

Step by step, day by day, I continue to walk by faith, I continue to strive, not being moved by what I see, hear, or think, but by what I know to be the truth; that which is ordained and predestined. I am/can be somebody and I can and will make a difference in this world.

I won't give up and I won't give in.

"And let us not be weary in well doing: for in due season we shall reap, if we faint not."
Galatians 6:9 (KJV)

Maximize the moment, go the extra mile.

It is
Patience

The ability to endure waiting, delay or provocation without becoming angry or upset. It is knowing that my time will come, and that God has not forgotten me.

It is taking the word complain and its actions out of my life. It is never having to fold my arms or pat my feet.

I refuse to panic have anxiety attacks or stress myself out, instead, I will be still and rest in the promises I have from the Father through the Word.

"To everything there is a season, and a time to every purpose under the heaven." Ecclesiastes 3:1 (KJV)

A challenge is a stimulant to grow and it builds strength with an optimistic attitude.

It is
Vision

It is perception, a mental picture, and my imagination, what I see. It is the dreamer impregnated with a dream of destiny.

It's being able to see what others can't or don't.

It is knowing that where I am right now in life is just preparation, or training ground for where I'm going.

It is the ability to see the good in the midst of the bad.

It is the ability to see it finished when I haven't even started.

I see it, I believe it, and there I will achieve it.

"Where there is no vision, the people perish:..."
Proverbs 29:18 (KJV)

A mirror is the truth it reflects, what is there in its original form. What is your mirror showing you? Are you happy with what you see? If not, make changes.

_____
_____
_____
_____
_____
_____
_____
_____
_____
_____
_____
_____
_____
_____
_____
_____

It is Creativeness

To be inspired ambitious and driven by one's thoughts.

It is being an original inventory of something great, or improving something that already exists.

It is the ability to see beyond seeing and hear beyond hearing.

Today, I will tap into the creative part of my soul, which is the Creator Himself within me, and see what original thoughts I can come up with.

My heart is indicting a good matter: My heart is overflowing with a beautiful thought.
Psalm 45:1a (KJV, Living)

The best way to predict your future is to create it.

It is Talent/Gifts

It is the natural ability to do something well, the formula, and the knowhow. It is your passion in life. Whether it is singing, dancing, designing, public speaking, etc. What do you do well? What do you have a heart for? That is your gift, your talent.

I will stop making excuses and work my passion.

"And unto one he gave five talents, to another two, and to another one; to every man according to his several ability; and straightway took his journey."
Matthew 25:15 (KJV)

"....but every man hath his proper gift of God, one after this manner; and another after that."
I Corinthians 7:7 (KJV)

"A man's gift maketh room for him, and bringeth him before great men." Proverbs 18:16 (KJV)

If you accept failure, accept it as a stepping stone to growth, as a measuring stick for what needs to be increased, but never accept it as defeat.

It is Courage

It is boldness, backbone and guts. It's being afraid but courageous at the same time.

It's the ability to stand-alone when others are afraid to take a stand for what they believe.

It's the nerve to speak up and out when others are quiet. To speak against injustices.

It's facing death in the face without trembling.

It's walking in dark places with no flashlight trusting only in your spirit to guide you.

I refuse to be afraid or intimidated by anything or anybody.

"Our heart is not turned back neither have our steps declined from thy way;" Psalm 44:18 (KJV)

Survival breeds confidence.

It is
Love

It is what God saw, and what he took from Himself to create me.

It is an Appreciation and respect for life. An appreciation for who I am, and for whom God has made me, knowing that He didn't make any mistakes but did a perfect and complete work.

It is the miracle of breathing. Know that every moment I am alive with every breath I take it is an opportunity for me to "Be."

It is true allegiance to Him who created me to fulfill His purpose for my life.

I am a story entitled "Love" that is being written every day and tomorrow somebody will be blessed by my story, so I will from this day be mindful of what I write on my pages.

"Now the end of the commandment is charity out of a pure heart, and of a good conscience, and of faith unfeigned;" I Timothy 1:5 (KJV)

Look for what is missing. Many know how to improve what's there, few can see what isn't there.

It is Forgiveness

It is the ability to release someone from the dungeon of my heart. It is to pardon one totally that the offense never happened. It is when I allow grace to be the true judge, that I might be free of the weight/burden.

Today I will forgive every person who has ever hurt, violated, intimidated, or raped me emotionally or physically.

I also forgive myself for holding on to bitterness, unforgiveness, and hurts of the past.

"Put on there, as the elect of God, holy and beloved, bowels of mercies, kindness, humbleness of mind, meekness, long-suffering; Forbearing one another, and forgiving one another, if any man have a quarrel against any; even as Christ forgave you, so also do ye."
Colossians 3:12-13 (KJV)

Eliminate the things that don't serve a healthy purpose in your life. Erase your dependency on whatever does not give you liberation and elevation.

This is His promise to you.

"For your shame ye shall have double; and for confusion they shall rejoice in their portion; therefore in their land they shall possess the double; everlasting joy shall be unto them." Isaiah 61:7 (KJV)

They were terribly insulted and horribly mistreated; now they will be greatly blessed and joyful forever.

"Instead of your [former] shame you shall have a twofold recompense; instead of dishonor and reproach [your people] shall rejoice in their portion. Therefore in their land they shall possess double [what they had forfeited]; everlasting joy shall be theirs." Isaiah 61:7 (AMP)

So do you have it?

Yes you do!!

"According as his divine power hath given unto us all things that pertain unto life and godliness, through the knowledge of him that hath called us to glory and virtue;"
2 Peter 1:3 (KJV)

We all have it but we must tap into it.

My sister, my brother, there is a CHAMPION inside you who is full of greatness who desires to be set free.

He is the voice you sometimes hear who whispers words of strength saying,

Stand! Fight! Don't give up!

He says I "Am" = "IT" don't quit!

The mere fact that you are still here after all you've been through tells me you have "IT!"

You are a fighter, a true warrior!

God made you tough, he knew that you would be able to take anything that life dished out to you and survive, so get up and move forward.

Now that I know what "IT" is, how do I tap into it?

By recognizing and acknowledging there is greatness/God inside you.

"You are of God, little children, and have overcome them: because greater is he that is in you, than he that is in the world."
I John 4:4 (KJV)

Through communication with him.

"Pray without ceasing."
I Thessalonians 5:17 (KJV)

"If any of you lack wisdom, let him ask of God, that giveth to all men liberally, and upbraideth not; and it shall be given him." James 1:5 (KJV)

Through communication with self.

"And David was greatly distressed; for the people spake of stoning him, because the soul of all the people was grieved, every man for his sons and for his daughters; but David encouraged himself in the Lord his God." I Samuel 30:6 (KJV)

Remembering the Word says, "Thou art snared with the words of thy mouth, thou art taken with the words of thy mouth."
Proverbs 6:2 (KJV)

So be careful what you are saying.

You were born at an appointed time for a divine reason far greater than you can imagine, therefore I challenge you to read and sign the promise.

The Promise

I Promise to love who God made me, knowing that I am special, I am unique, one of a kind, knowing that God did not make a mistake when he created me. I promise to be who God made me to be, I will not try to be like anybody else.

I promise to fulfill his plan for my life that I might make a difference in someone else's life.

Signature below:

_____

Ruth Wilson is the pastor and founder of the Shekinah Glory International Ministries located in Louisville, KY. She is on a personal mission to expose the enemy for who and what he is; a LIAR and a THIEF.

She believes that once we know the truth we can't help but be free.

"And ye shall know the truth, and the truth shall make you free."
John 8:32 (KJV)

God is not a respecter of persons. What He does for one, He will do for another; He'll do it for you.

It is our prayer that this book has been an eye opener, life, and motivation for you to move forward.

Let us know, tell someone else, or if you would like to order additional copies send all correspondence to:

Dr. Ruth Wilson
P. O. Box 133
Louisville, KY 40201

Email us at:
dauparoom@yahoo.com

www.ingramcontent.com/pod-product-compliance
Lightning Source LLC
Chambersburg PA
CBHW051713090426
42736CB00013B/2677